I WORE THIS DRESS
TODAY FOR YOU, MOM

I WORE THIS DRESS
TODAY FOR YOU, MOM

poems
on motherhood

Kim Dower

Red Hen Press | *Pasadena, CA*

Book design by Mark E. Cull

Library of Congress Cataloging-in-Publication Data

Names: Dower, Kim, author.
Title: I wore this dress today for you, Mom : poems on motherhood / Kim Dower.
Description: First edition. | Pasadena, CA : Red Hen Press, [2022]
Identifiers: LCCN 2021031787 (print) | LCCN 2021031788 (ebook) | ISBN
   9781636280233 (hardcover) | ISBN 9781636280882 (tradepaper) |
   ISBN 9781636280240 (epub)
Subjects: LCGFT: Poetry.
Classification: LCC PS3604.O9395 I52 2022 (print) | LCC PS3604.O9395
   (ebook) | DDC 811/.6—dc23
LC record available at https://lccn.loc.gov/2021031787

The National Endowment for the Arts, the Los Angeles County Arts Commission, the Ahmanson Foundation, the Dwight Stuart Youth Fund, the Max Factor Family Foundation, the Pasadena Tournament of Roses Foundation, the Pasadena Arts & Culture Commission and the City of Pasadena Cultural Affairs Division, the City of Los Angeles Department of Cultural Affairs, the Audrey & Sydney Irmas Charitable Foundation, the Meta & George Rosenberg Foundation, the Albert and Elaine Borchard Foundation, the Adams Family Foundation, Amazon Literary Partnership, the Sam Francis Foundation, and the Mara W. Breech Foundation partially support Red Hen Press.

    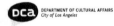

First Edition
Published by Red Hen Press
www.redhen.org
Printed in Canada

For my mother and Nana
and for my son
each of whom taught me
the meaning of unconditional love

and

For all mothers
and for everyone who's ever had
a mother

CONTENTS

I WORE THIS DRESS
TODAY FOR YOU, MOM

"I will look after you and I will look after anybody you say needs to be looked after, any way you say. I am here. I brought my whole self to you. I am your mother."
—Maya Angelou

"If you listen to [your children], somehow you are able to free yourself from baggage and vanity and all sorts of things, and deliver a better self, one that you like. The person that was in me that I liked best was the one my children seemed to want."
—Toni Morrison

"My mother wanted me to be her wings, to fly as she never quite had the courage to do. I love her for that. I love the fact that she wanted to give birth to her own wings."
—Erica Jong

"One thing about having a baby is that each step of the way you simply cannot imagine loving him any more than you already do, because you are bursting with love, loving as much as you are humanly capable of—and then you do, you love him even more."
—Anne Lamott

SHE'S NEVER TRUSTED HAPPINESS

Maybe it was something her mother said
one morning as the young girl dipped
her donut into a glass of whole milk
powdered sugar still on her lips her mother
tells her, don't get used to this

DIFFERENT MOTHERS

I've read about the ones who garden,
teach their daughters to cut a rose
just above the thorns—so a fresh bud will pop up
like toast in time for breakfast.

These different mothers show their daughters
how to plant tomato seeds in the damp earth,
tingle when the first green fruit appears,
and when they explode into deep red

pick them off the vine, slice them
in their sunny kitchens. These are mothers
whose daughters learn through smells
of lakes, weeds, pastry dough,

have memories of lightning bugs in jars
mothers have poked holes into.
These are different mothers.
I am not one. My mother

didn't know about soil or earth worms.
City mothers, we know about bus routes, restaurants,
Broadway, the people on the eighth floor.
Mine taught me to accessorize, bring the ideal

hostess gift, have my keys in hand
when I enter the building. I have no daughter,
but my son can look anyone in the eye, tell them
what he's thinking. We eat tomatoes

from the grocery. Our roses are store-bought.
Different mothers *sound* better
and I think about what might have been:
calling to the birds, naming the stars,

fingers locked together while hiking
on hidden trails, cleaning homegrown mint
before placing it in tea before bed.
I'll flag a cab instead.

I WORE THIS DRESS TODAY FOR YOU, MOM,

breezy floral, dancing with color
soft, silky, flows as I walk.
Easter Sunday, and you always liked

to get dressed, go for brunch, *maybe*
there's a good movie playing somewhere?
Wrong religion, we were not churchgoers,

but New Yorkers who understood the value
of a parade down Fifth Avenue, bonnets
in lavender, powder blues, pinks, hues

of spring, the hope it would bring.
We had no religion, but we did have
noodle kugel, grandparents, dads

who could fix fans, reach the china
on the top shelf, carve the turkey.
That time has passed. You were the last

to go, mom, and I still feel bad I never
got dressed up for you like you wanted me to.
I had things, things to do. But today in LA,

hot the way you liked it—those little birds
you loved to see flitting from tree to tree—
just saw one, a twig in its mouth, preparing

a bed for its baby—might still be an egg,
I wish you were here. I've got a closet filled
with dresses I need to show you.

LETTER TO MY SON

Dementia runs in the family, so if I can't think of a name or a place, a moment everyone else can vividly recall, I feel afraid. Useless. Ashamed. You see, I don't want anyone to carry me into another room so I can get a view of a tree or remind me what a tree is or tell me what I'm sipping from is called a straw. I've seen it all before. My grandfather didn't know he was eating a banana—only that someone had to peel it for him, and that thing, that peel, had to be thrown away. I'm not saying it's certain I will have dementia, but if I do, please know this: I won't be mad if you don't take care of me. I won't even know that you're not. Tell me everything's okay, and I will believe you. Tell me there's a bird on a branch outside my window, even if there is no window, and I will imagine he's singing to me. Once when a storm was coming, my mother looked up at the sky, told me God was punching the clouds to make rain pour out. She never even believed in God. The point is this: I may not know exactly who you are when you come to visit. I may be confused. But when I hold your hand it will all come back in waves: rocking you in my arms when you were a baby, your little seltzer voice, my heart flooding my body with joy every morning you jumped in my bed. I will not be angry like some people with dementia can get. I've never been good at angry. I will not peel the yellow paper off the wall or bite my caregiver. Play a few rounds of blackjack with me. You deal. I will smile each time I get a picture card. Tell me I've hit twenty-one even if I bust. Use real chips, have party drinks with ice that clinks, a cocktail napkin with which to dab my lips.

DUBONNET

My grandmother would sip a juice glass
of Dubonnet—dark purplish red, color
of her identical twin sister's lips, the one
who stayed behind in Russia, every night
as she prepared the roast, Mike Douglas
blasting on the television, my grandfather snoring,
the apartment a swirl of garlic, chicken fat,
boiled secrets, longing flooding the rooms
like sunlight. Once she offered me a taste:
Some people like it with a twist of lemon,
but I like it plain. I was seven. My tongue burned
through the sweetness. I floated into the next room
without moving. I would dress up in her black
cloth cape, sequined ladybug pin, clump around
in her tiny pumps. She was the size of Thumbelina.
I remember the warm baths, splashes of Jean Nate,
the pink chenille bathrobe, photo of them as girls
hanging in the dark hallway. My grandmother
told me her name just once: *Tanya*, this identical her,
living on the other side of the world, another Nana
saying goodnight to another me.

GAME OVER

I squirted too much mustard on my hotdog
and now I can't eat it, I tell my friend at the game.
That's why God made napkins, he tells me—

wipe it off. I tell him I knew God made mustard
but didn't know He also made napkins. I tell him
once the mustard gets soaked up by the bun

it's game over, even napkins won't help.
He's disturbed. I can see in his face he's mad
I wasted a perfectly decent hotdog and worse,

now I'm doubting God. *When did you stop
believing in Him?* he asks me, his face twisted
like the pretzel I'm about to put mustard on.

Did I *ever* believe in God? Was God peeking
through the window, up there in Laurel Canyon
when my son was conceived? Was He in my belly

when they sliced it open so they could lift my baby
out of his warm, private ocean? Was God in my son's
hands when he pitched a perfect game at the Pan?

My friend's still talking . . . *I was an altar boy,*
he continues . . . *you don't forget the Eucharist,
wearing the crisp cassock, snuffing out candles*

as the priest consecrates bread and wine . . . you
don't forget ringing the bells until someone you love
dies, then it's game over. He tells me these things

our shoulders touching as Manny hits deep
into left field, the men on base run their hearts out,
thousands in the stands praying, *please* God, *please,*

get the run, win the game, as the mustard hardens
on my cold dog, bun stiff, I slip it under my seat
with God's blessing as the first man slides safely to home.

CLIVE CHRISTIAN No. 1

The cosmetics lady sprays me
with the world's most expensive perfume
as I pull open the heavy glass door
Neiman's, Beverly Hills. I'm here to buy

a gift, she sprays me with notes of plum,
pineapple, white peach—*it'll linger twenty-four hours*
it's what Katie Holmes wore the night
she married Tom Cruise—now on me,

jasmine tangerine headachy, smelling
like Katie under the covers, imagining
Tom in the bathroom not coming
out. I keep nuzzling my wrist as I browse

through men's scarves, falling in love
with myself, wondering if *I* should've worn
Clive Christian No.1 on *my* wedding night,
not residue of Bain de Soleil left from the day

poolside in Santa Barbara. I'm still searching
for my signature scent: rose oil tinged
with poison, weekend aphrodisiac, forbidden
sweat. I remember how I used to test

my mother's, kept on the blue depressed-glass
tray on her dresser. I'd spray up into the air
of her bedroom, wave the fragrance onto my face,
think how my friends' mothers were perfume-free,

used cold cream, Vaseline, never smelled
more than clean, and on the way out, empty
handed, she zaps me again, this time she hits me
with bergamot, lime, Sicilian mandarin, thyme,

it's what Sylvester Stallone wears, she tells me,
it'll linger at least a week, people backing away,
disgusted, as I exit through the main floor:
a woman smelling like a famous man.

GOODBYE TO JAMES GARNER

Fans loved him as *Rockford*, *Maverick*,
a man's man, had your back, cool,
did the right thing. I loved him
for being Doris Day's husband
in a movie I cut class to see,
fifth grade, played at the Riviera,
only old men and me during the day,
went alone, told no one, but I had a gigantic
crush on him, he was an OB/GYN,
she was a mom, marriage in jeopardy,
couples in movies stayed together in the sixties
while out there it was all falling apart,
women poised to flip their lives, months away
from marching into a world of miniskirts, riots,
shame, pillbox hats, flinging our boxy pink suit jackets
and pumps into the sunset, not even James Garner
could have saved us, and this week, now, more unrest
more wars unfolding, I'm stuck on the headline
James Garner Dead. When I was ten, I needed a man
I could count on—even one holding aces and eights.

NO ONE BLEEDS FOREVER

for Grace Paley

They sat on the bench—Washington Square Park
Grace and my mother, before I was born
my mother with my older brother,
Grace with her own.
Quirky, my mother told me, years later,
when I asked, *she was so different before
she wrote her stories*, before my mother
would move uptown into her new life.
They had the Bronx in common—the place
no one wants to admit they're from.

Grace would wear *these hats* she'd tell me,
we had so much to talk about the babies, those feelings,
she was *bossy*, a young female writer, 1950
sounds so romantic now, but Grace had to scoop
her children up and give them baths,
just like my mother, had to stick thermometers in them,
feed them green purées from jars, had rough hands
from washing out diapers.
And, like her characters, she had hope, just like my
mother who always believed, *no one bleeds forever.*

BIRTH

She can feel the bulk of him:
a three story home parked
under her rib cage.

She can feel them reach
inside her guts
to pull him out,

no pain, just numb tugging,
wet cries from inside
where he lived for nine months,

her tiny kangaroo
waiting like a wish
struggling to come true.

She feels him stretching out,
one last kick to connect them.
She will miss his breathing

into her dreams.
Will he miss her food
invading his?

She tries to picture life
after birth, after they take him
from her body,

her second heart
delivered into heavy arms,
paralyzed by the block

they shot into her spine.
At first, all she sees
are his long fingers,

nails razor-sharp, tissue paper
she runs across her lips
tasting the salt of life.

PREGNANT

In my dream last night I whispered in Meryl Streep's ear
that I was pregnant. *That's great*, she said, her eyes
searching my face. But *I'm sixty*, I whispered. *Oh my*,
she said, touching my cheek, asking who the father was.
My husband, I told her. *Thank god*, she said, but we parted
uncomfortably, me not even knowing her well in the first place,
so I had hoped to make a good impression. When I met the doctor,
I was unsure how I felt, would he be able to handle this kind of
older pregnancy, what kind of mother to a tween would I be at
seventy, would I still be doing carpool in my golden years, choosing
prom dresses from catalogs side by side with my medical
equipment journals. The horrors of old age juxtaposed with
cheerful youth seemed insurmountable and so I consulted
my best friend Janice. She was very blonde in my dream with
peach complexion, turquoise earrings, looked like a sweet
nursery school–teacher. She was concerned but steady,
asked me if I'd consider an abortion and I burst into tears,
the hot kind that burn as they roll down and if skin on your
face is already chapped from cold days of long walks those
tears are truly unpleasant, so we didn't say the word abortion
again, not that I have a moral problem with it, but if there's life
inside me I want to see what kind of life it is, I want to hold it
at the end of that long day, I want to make it grilled cheese,
swing it into the sky on a beach day, I want to read it *Where's Waldo?*.

THE THINGS I DO IN MY CAR

no one knows
the things I do in my car

my traveling LA secret circus
cruising around lucky I haven't killed anyone

that swerve to the left not looking must
be careful there's something on my leg an itch

someone to my right looking in
you're the only one I'll tell but once I cried

reached under my skirt to feel I was alive
slow roll through the red

not even my therapist can know
the things I do in my car

skin-popping words onto my arm
tangerine juice rolling down my thigh

I solved a murder made love to a stranger
fell for a loser wet my eyeliner brush with my tongue

drove my baby to sleep years ago
I'd ride around at dusk waiting for his crying to subside

he screeched as I wound through the canyon
breathing in my future as he'd drift away

his fever dreams melting into Sundays spent
curling down the California incline watched the ocean

follow me north took my dress off cranked up the sixties
blasted the news out of the sunroof flashed

on the subway I used to ride back then stuck inside
suffocating black breezes no secrets no rays hitting me

no top down no windows just darkness grazing
the shoulders of strangers

hoping to get there safe destination Fifty-Seventh Street
sticky floating people up on the sidewalk stepping faster

racing the cars hot from exhaust
no ocean just lights red green busses yellow heat

not from sun but bodies
drenched in their own distress

the smell of fumes bouncing off the eastern sky
so low I could catch them in my mouth

not the high western sky where now I drive for an endless day
racing the sea where the things I do in my car

only matter to me because no one knows
no one can see

THE COUPLE NEXT DOOR

The couple next door reads all day long.
I can see them from our adjoining hotel patios
high above the sea.

The couple next door sits
at a round white plastic table on hard chairs,
their books touching as they

turn their pages at the same time.
I listen for any sounds they might make:
soft cough, sigh of joy, but

I hear nothing except for southbound traffic
on the Pacific Coast Highway, distant
waves, morning sounds of housekeepers

cleaning the grounds below our deck.
The man's book looks fat; I can see him
thick glasses, brand new cap

staring intently into the page.
I never see him smile, so I know the book is not funny.
I never see him shake his head, so I know the book does not

confuse him, but he suddenly lifts his head
looks out at the ocean, puts his hand over his mouth.
The woman looks content like her book understands her:

it's about something she knows too well—
bringing up children, watching them grow,
saying goodbye.

I brought books too but prefer watching them:
wonder how they arrived at this place
where reading in silence carries them through the day.

SARDINES

We go for Portuguese, my friend and I,
family restaurant by the beach,
nice tables, they bring olives without

us asking, even the bread tastes good.
Do you like sardines? I ask her. *I love
those little chubby ones that come in a tin,*

*they're brain food, you know, and great
for your skin.* So we tell the waiter
(nice young guy, accent, wedding ring),

and he delivers us three huge sardines,
not looking like any we've ever seen,
tails like fireplace brushes. We tackle

these shining fish, open them, remove
their delicate spines, fork out the salty
meat, concentrate on each morsel,

careful not to swallow the fragile splinters
like warnings on our tongues, start to talk,
what's new, our boys all grown, spit out

what we don't trust: bones, words, *seen it all,
haven't we? if only we knew then*—a sharp
fragment sliding down my throat—*remember*

our trip to Catalina—we lost them in the soda
machine room, mine was only three for God's sake,
we were frantic, hotel people running around,

walkie talkies—I'm chewing faster, choking
on pieces of fish face, my friend watching,
It's the wholeness of the sardine really turns me

off, she says, pushing her plate as I scoop out
the second eyeball, slip it into my mouth.
It's the *wholeness* that excites me: skin, guts,

brains. I want to taste the murky world
beyond my future, I want to eat what stares at me
in darkness, what has already seen its own death,

and when the waiter asks if we want dessert,
if there will be anything else, I tell him yes:
more eyes, please. I want to eat more eyes.

EVERYBODY LOVES DINNER

When I walk into my mother's house
I see a pot on the stove high flame

charring the sides
she thinks she's boiling

water but the water has evaporated
like a ghost fleeing the scene

leaving the bottom scalded, a blackness
that cannot be reversed.

It was only a matter of months. You see,
she was very careful in the kitchen

taught me the same:
check the pilot lights, smell for gas

unclutter the space where you cook
simple things like this she taught me

so last week when I visited when I saw
the blue flame hugging the sides of that old pot

sitting too close to the Kleenex I'd hand her
sobbing as she watched TV

so much violence, was it always like this,
sit down, darling, let's eat, everybody loves dinner

but there was no food, nothing there to cook
I hadn't brought a thing, what was I thinking

but we smiled, held hands, I changed the channel
she told me she felt full and was ready for bed.

MY MOTHER HAS A FITFUL SLEEP

My mother has a fitful sleep,
dreams of car rides that never end,
people pushing to evacuate the building,

swans inside of swans, words trying to form
in the shape of giant *O*s, bunnies shaking
dust off the tips of their ears. My mother

has a fitful sleep, she's in the hospital,
can't eat, use a straw, can't hum *Impossible You*.
Her body tries to roll over, damp as a squeegee

after a ride across the windshield of my dad's
old green Ford. She always had earaches on long
trips south, heading from New York to Florida,

me stretched across the backseat reading
To Kill a Mockingbird, parents smoking Camels,
bickering where to eat, she had to pee, he tried

to please, those biscuits in South Carolina,
the red-haired waitress at the diner. My mother
has a fitful sleep, hears the groans of the man

she once married, my father, his hands like trout
on a hook, heat hissing off him like the radiator
their towels would dry on in the old apartment.

My mother has a fitful sleep, legs twitching,
she nibbles her arm as if it were buttered toast,
her body releasing mist from the hurricane inside her.

MY MOTHER WANTS EXTRA CRISP BACON

I take my mother for a ride.
She needs to get out of the house,
see something green, smell
summer air; she's going
mad. I drive her
through Beverly Hills.
Mom, I say, pointing out
a gigantic Tudor, *look at that mansion!*
I say it again because she's deaf.
Now I'm yelling,
LOOK AT THAT MANSION,
she's happy to see the mansion, likes
"all those windows."
How many people do you think live in there,
she asks me. *Do you think they have servants?*
She's getting hungry; wants a BLT.
She'd order those when I was a kid,
always demanding extra crisp bacon,
would complain, send it back,
I'd be embarrassed, protective,
look upset—like why didn't it come crisp
in the first place—why did she have
so many disappointments,
never satisfied by my father's gifts,
that freakish mink wrap, for example, hated it,
he was crushed, you could see it laying
like a dead animal in the road

under the Christmas tree for weeks
covered by dried pine needles.
I touched it once, it was soft, like her cheek
or her arm. She'd cry at the drop of a hat
if you hit the right nerve, which I knew
how to do but never dared.
I take my mother in the car because she can't walk,
needs to get out, see something lively, fresh,
growing, chat with me about houses others live in,
why don't we live there,
always wanting what she never had,
always dragging me along for the ride.

GAIL EXPLAINS ABOUT MY MOTHER'S GLASSES

Remember, Gail tells me, *if your mother
can't find her glasses, they may be in the fridge.*

She tells me this without judgment or sadness;
she tells me as if she's reminding me that people

put anything anywhere when they get old, forgetful,
when they no longer care about seeing anything

anywhere. I'm grateful to have this valuable clue:
I've spent hours on my hands, knees searching

under my mother's couch, squeezing my arm
under her burgundy chair, feeling for the metal touch

of her tired eyeglasses. These are different
from the harlequins she wore coming home from work

on the Broadway bus or on Madison Avenue, her heels
getting stuck in the sidewalk cracks, her skirt blowing up

like Marilyn's. These are not the glasses she flung
across the room one morning when I was young

after a hushed phone call; not the ones she left on the side
of the tub covering *The Feminine Mystique.*

These aren't the horn rims she wore to our graduations,
or took off when reading to my son. Good to know

when she calls me in the late afternoon, numb from napping,
television blasting, me at work absorbed in other people's

problems, or right before I take my first sip of wine at dinner,
good to know when she calls to tell me her glasses are missing,

that probably a man broke into her place and stole them,
you must come now and see what else he's taken,

I'll know they're in the fridge, icy as the ginger ale that settles
her stomach, stiff as the roast beef, going bad by the day.

BOTTLED WATER

I go to the corner liquor store
for a bottle of water, middle
of a hectic day, must get out
of the office, stop making decisions,
quit obsessing does my blue skirt clash
with my hot-pink flats; should I get
my mother a caregiver or just put her
in a home; and I pull open the glass
refrigerator door, am confronted
by brands—Arrowhead, Glitter Geyser,
Deer Park, spring, summer, winter water,
and clearly the bosses of bottled water:
Real Water and smartwater—how different
will they taste? If I drink smartwater
will I raise my IQ but be less authentic?
If I choose Real Water will I no longer
deny the truth, but will I attract confused,
needy people who'll take advantage
of my realness by dumping their problems
on me, and will I be too stupid to help them
sort through their murky dilemmas?
I take no chances, buy them both,
sparkling smart, purified real, drain both bottles,
look around to see is anyone watching?
I'm now brilliantly hydrated.
Both real *and* smart, my insides bubble

with compassion and intelligence
as I walk the streets with a new swagger,
knowing the world is mine.

LUNCH WITH GLORIA

First we compare sweaters: rayon, cashmere,
agree we only want to wear what's super soft,

no more itchy for us, ever. She tells me
she loves linen but I say, *no! Too scratchy,*

stiff, unyielding. If linen could talk it would say things
that hurt. *You just have to know how to care for linen,*

Gloria tells me, inviting me to touch her blouse.
Feel how soft. It wrinkles terribly, but I don't care:

it's a fabric of special qualities—complex, rare
one can hardly complain when it knots up.

We talk necklaces, how we want ours to tell stories
about the people who gave them to us, which occasions.

She shows me hers—a ring on a chain from a young man
she'll always love. He's gone now but never gone

from her heart. I show her the locket hiding behind my shirt.
I got this for myself after my son was born, rose gold,

tiny ruby, just one eye peeking out of the stroller,
my baby's face, the size of a sigh.

THE SALVATION ARMY WON'T TAKE THE FUTON

Because it's not a couch, not a bed,
The Salvation Army won't take the futon
from my mother's apartment. It has to be one

or the other, not in between, like my mother,
who's alive, but not really here.
The Salvation Army truck is taking the stuff

she'll no longer need: blue porcelain jar lamp, end
table where she kept my phone number, her tissues,
hard candies, burnt orange velour chair from where

she watched TV, argued with the news, critiqued
Diane Sawyer's wardrobe—*too much beige.*
I'm moving her to a place where ladies' faces break

into smiles for no reason. The movers lug her things
onto their truck, each piece caked with the kind of dust
that settles after we give up. They don't know she's trapped

in a board and care, propped up by pillows someone
recently died leaning against. I beg him to let the rules slide.
Who'd ever know it's a futon? The luscious fabric,

the pattern? Who would ever question this wasn't a couch?
My mother just liked the word, that it could be both,
she liked knowing it didn't have to be one or the other.

BOARD AND CARE CLOCK

My mother tells me she needs a clock,
is unsure of the time when she wakes

after a late afternoon nap ever since
she's been in *this place*. I tell her, *look—*

look up there—point to the clock, round,
clear as her grandchildren's faces,

show her the second hand, how it ticks
on the wall above the TV, but she says, *no*,

she doesn't like that clock, wants a smaller,
more intimate clock to sit beside like a friend

in the park. She wants time to be hers alone,
like the chocolates I bring she won't share

with the other ladies in hats who sit politely,
all dying for the same thing: a reason to care

what time it is as the seconds gather like dots
on an impressionist painting, grey, shadowy

soft edges of intermingling minutes, creating
the illusion of color, light, the culmination of life.

I LOST MY MOTHER AT BLOOMINGDALE'S

I had no idea I tell the authorities she just left the store
but you were right there could have stopped her
I was in the dressing room trying on a frilly bathing suit

the salesman fiddling with the straps adjusting them to fit
my top while my mother escaped onto the street
no ID money sense of where she was started walking

up Central Park West trying to find the old nursing home
she put her father back then when I lived so far away
I remember once seeing him in bed blank eyes deck of cards

in his giant chapped hands half-eaten banana by his bedside
smile slowly coming from deep inside when he saw me at the door
like my mother's smile when she sees me enter *her* nursing home

and now my mother's searching for her father for clues
about who she is ever was I took her out took a chance had no idea
she'd leave my side the bathing suit was almost perfect what if

they can't find her what if she vanishes into a refurbished
brownstone
stairwell her dress on backwards label showing lost forever after
her last outing shopping with me it's what we did what we loved until

THE PEOPLE IN THE HEALTH FOOD STORE

The people in the health food store
don't look healthy, which is why they're here.
I'm here to get carrot chips, craving crunch,

flavor, after visiting my mother at the home
where flavor only appears in faint whiffs
of memory, where people in wheelchairs

suspiciously eye the applesauce on their trays
delivered by chubby nurses in red scrubs,
pictures of ponies or baby elephants stitched

onto pockets that contain their syringes and keys
to the lounge. The people in the health food store
look dirty, wear spandex, have spaces between

their teeth, prowl the aisles for natural
supplements, inner peace, Ola Loa energy drinks,
so only the other losers will die, not them,

not after they cleanse their bodies of all
impurities, destroy lingering negative thoughts:
what if my baby never learns to talk, what if

I suddenly forget how to walk, what if the earth
sucks me deep into hell, like the hell my mother
lives in, where when I visit she asks me,

Who put me here, when did this happen?
It was only yesterday she sipped martinis
on the rooftops of Manhattan, so it's no wonder I run

for the health food store, fill my basket with Miracle
Cream to rub in every pore, stock up on Wrinkle
Warrior, buy a year's supply of brain enhancers

so when it's *my* turn to stare out the window wearing
floral-patterned daytime pajamas, I'll remember
who I am, who I was, who I once loved.

SLICE OF MOON

There's a slice of moon
left over in the sky, a sliver
of carnival glass wedged

into the milky blue,
as if the Gods
had a midnight party,

couldn't finish it all,
left a piece of moon
for us, barely throbbing

in the morning light,
a crescent of white
hanging onto the sober sky.

Why is it still up there
on this new day?
Its job, to taunt darkness,

burn through the night
like heaven's candle,
igniting our dreams,

should be over. Why
does this moon persist?
The sun sets as it's meant to,

leaves the sky gracefully,
falling into the arms
of the ocean.

We can trust it to disappear
so the sky can darken,
so we may rest, rocked

by the pale memory
of motion, rocked by the song
our mothers sang or never sang.

Dying is Not Black,

Erica tells me,
from her dying mother's
bedside, her mother
who still rejoices
in her daughter's colors
reaches out to touch
as did mine
at the very end
her eyes gray
blue
turning
green
the color I feared.
I love that color on you,
my mother said
the night she died,
reaching her shaky hand
to touch the pink
of my scarf. *I prefer*
earth tones, you know,
for myself, that is, but on you . . .
and off she drifted
an evening shadow
fading into shallow
breathing
as I closed
her blue eyes
for the first time.

THE DELIVERY MAN

would drive his little van down the street,
slide open the door, his face obscured
by hanging clothes draped in plastic bags,
take out his penis and masturbate
as he watched us play handball against
the Party Cake wall. We were nine or ten
maybe eleven and we knew when he drove by
what it would mean. Some of us stopped to watch,
could only see the quick movement of his hand,
but once I saw it all. It was like being transfixed
by a crash on the side of the road—ashamed
to want to take in the suffering of others, yet
bewitched by the horrifying images.
His grunts were obscured by the traffic,
but if you went close enough to his truck
you could hear the groan of relief when he was done.
He wore an oversized raincoat just like the joke.
We never told our dads but our moms knew.
They saw him, too. He's exposing himself,
my mother explained. No one made me look
but I couldn't turn away—paralyzed by fear
and the excitement of repulsion—of knowing
it was wrong but needing to see how he
did this thing, wanting to be his audience
in a sticky white mess of daylight.

SOLACE

Solaced by an abundance of whisky, champagne and cigars,
he always bounced back, restoring and recreating himself through
intensely active immersion in one or another of his varied interests . . .
—Robert Kuttner, *New York Times* Book Review, 23 Oct. 1988

My mother passed away in her sleep last night
after we all had Thanksgiving dinner, and I'm trying
to find solace. When I looked the word up to make sure
I was searching for the right thing, this is what I found.
Seems an awful lot of information to explain a word
that means to console, to make cheerful, or to amuse.
After reading it I thought I might never find solace
because I don't drink whisky, don't smoke cigars,
champagne makes me dizzy. I wondered, too, who
is this man who always bounced back and what *are*
his varied interests? Do I share any of them? I found
a little solace today by eating random foods I'd otherwise
never touch. I had a very rich meat sauce on whole wheat
spaghetti, a glass of red wine, this is not uncommon,
but then gorged myself on chocolate-covered dried fruit,
popping them in my mouth, fistfuls of bliss, sips of wine,
then forkfuls of salad, tart dressing, cucumbers, olives,
feta cheese, and it all began to taste the same, just the need
to taste *something* and not remember that I no longer
have a mother I can call or see or worry about.
Where's this solace that so many people are mentioning to me?
Does it exist? Let this stranger have an abundance of whisky.
I'll have my chocolate-covered dried fruit and let's see

who'll throw up first. Get him on the phone for me, I yelled to no one.
Let's see how long it took *him* to restore and recreate himself through
intensely active immersion in one or another of his varied interests.
I'll give it a try: a little air hockey tonight, some online blackjack,
followed by shrieking an ABBA song at the moon plastered against
the black ice sky. I will find that solace even if I have to scrape
it off the walls with my nails, and I'll bounce back like a handball
off the side of the building where I played after school,
where my mother sat on the stoop with her friends smoking
Kent cigarettes, talking about the war, their sons, marriage, grief,
watched us yelling not to run into the street. I will bounce back
in the same way I surrender to heartache: laying down,
letting the pain of loss wrap itself around me like a lead blanket,
protecting me from the radiation of saying goodbye.

LITTLE GLASS DISHES

Cleaning out my mother's cabinets
I spot them buried behind dusty mugs:
little glass dishes, set of twelve, thin

but hearty, like my grandmother we called
Nana, round, the size of a gigantic pancake,
the size of my grandfather's palm, a thistle

engraved around the side, been in my family
since the Depression, used for stuffed cabbage,
pirozhkis, a Chesterfield or two extinguished

in a plump baked apple, shrimp cocktail
in the better years, served to the family, to Hyman,
the boarder Nana took in, found him at the newsstand,

corner Ninety-Sixth and Central Park, liked his lefty politics,
lost his right leg in a war I'd never heard of,
had a wooden one he'd let me and my brother knock

if we were good. Now the dishes belong to me.
I took them when I moved my mother to the home.
There were other things—a garnet ring that never fit,

stack of letters I couldn't get myself to read—
but I wanted those dishes. They reminded me
of holidays when I was a girl, bundled in my camel hair

coat, back seat of my dad's green Ford, on our way
to apartment 3B where me and grandpa would play
gin rummy, chocolate bars stacked high on the cold

windowsill, listen as the dishes got cleared
to make room for the next course. That was many
meals ago. This morning when I scraped the food away,

ran my fingers over the magical glass, I could see
both sides of my hands. I could remember
all of us bumping into one another in that crowded

kitchen, feel the heat from the oven, smell the food
coming out see Nana's small hand shake as she sliced
the noodle kugel, crisp on top but never burnt.

How was your weekend,

the lab technician asks me
as she sticks the needle in my vein,
routine physical, blood rushing
up the tube as if being chased
out of my body. *Fine*, I tell her
all good, really good, did some things,
saw some people, ate out, got rid of shoes
I haven't worn in years, craved ice cream,
but had no one to go with, so I went by myself,
embarrassed ordering a mint chip cone
alone in the middle of a Saturday, got over it
when I took a bite, euphoric, no longer caring
that my son was too old to take for ice cream.
Wrote a letter to my dead mother but couldn't
read it at her grave because we cremated her
so I read it sitting at the kitchen table,
a photo of her propped up in front of me.
Sounds amazing, she says, my blood still flowing
up the tube, new one now as I'd filled up the first.
Where will they send my blood, and how
do they test for all the things they test for,
and what if they discover I have one
of a million diseases one could have, something
to confine me to bed for as many days, weekends
as I have left on this earth, or what if they find
nothing? Will I start to take pictures of my food
like a friend of mine does? He takes pictures

of what he's about to eat so he'll remember
what he put in his body, so if something goes
wrong he'll know it was the yellowtail swimming
in lime sauce or the ginger sorbet with one proud
blackberry perched on top. He keeps files of photos
so he'll never forget what he tasted, what filled him.
I want to taste the blood being drawn from my arm,
wonder if it would taste the same as my mother's.
What did you do this weekend, she asks
forgetting she already asked. *I had an ice cream cone,*
I tell her, *took a picture of it before it started to melt,*
licked a drop of blood still warm from a new cut,
read a letter to my mother at her grave.

THE GENE

Grace draws blood from my arm.
I don't feel a thing as I pump the red
rubber ball she places in my hand.

This is good, she says, the flow
is consistent, as if my blood is grateful
to come out, has a reason to fill the vial.

They will take it to a lab, run tests to see
if I have the gene that will change my life,
one my grandmother who died

of breast cancer may have passed
to my father on a dark night when he lay
in her womb, my embryo dad unaware

he was being nourished by what might
someday kill his daughter.
Are you Ashkenazi? Grace asks me,

like I would know, the needle stuck
in my arm, her question as foreign
as the idea that I could be carrying

a death-sentence gene, that my ovaries
might be time bombs
ready to bust my guts in two.

If I have the gene I might die sooner
than Grace unless she dies in an explosion
at a stadium watching baseball or running

in a terminal to catch a plane.
Her hand on my arm, my imagination
bleeds into my mind. If I have this gene

will I remove my breasts just to be safe,
or will I keep them as promises to myself
that something tragic will happen even though

it will anyway, with or without, I am bound to die
as is Grace, as did my father on the golf course
one smoggy day, not a gene that took him,

just his blood stopped flowing, his heart
gave out, the red rubber ball
could no longer pump.

EASTER SUNDAY

She'd always wished
this could *really* be her holiday

colored eggs, a basket of jellybeans
floating on fake grass, pastel ribbons

her mother laid out on her bed
(there'd be a soft bunny, too,

bright ears, black beads for eyes),
but where was the magical gold cross?

Jesus didn't belong to her
like he belonged to the ladies in mint

green coats, pouring into
St. Patrick's Cathedral hemorrhaging

rebirth, while she'd be at Tip Toe Inn
spreading Russian dressing

on her lean corned beef, her grandmother
in elbow length gloves, winter chill still

in the New York air, pretending she was in church
like Donna and her sisters, praying to be forgiven.

VISITING ELEANOR

Barbara, my childhood piano teacher
played Chopin like he was whispering
into her hands, all us kids from the building
had our Saturday morning lessons, apartment 6C,
our giddy fingers trotting in the key of G,
lifting high for Mozart, metronome ticking
as her coffee brewed, her sandy-haired husband
at the wooden breakfast table, mug, cigarette
tight in his hands, he was the man on the Winston
ads, I'd slide by him, eyes down on my way
to the bedroom where the shining black upright
Steinway sat facing Broadway, her daughter pirouetting
across the checkered linoleum floor, tiny yellow socks
collecting dust with each step, twirling to the music
we were all struggling so hard to learn how to play.
And here we are a lifetime later, arm in arm, walking
in the rain, joyous as a sonata on our way to Seventy-Second street,
visiting Eleanor, she calls it *the only statue of a woman
in the entire city*, tightening her grip, her bicep strong
as a ballerina's calf muscle, and it all comes back,
she and my mother close talking in our kitchen, Barbara's pink
mohair sweater, hair in rollers, the two of them always
wanting to put things behind them, the music of their motherhood,
beat of secrets, music of being someone's daughter. I still have
my music book filled with her notes: *moderate tempo, allegro,
practice! Here's where you get into trouble.*

SLEEP OVER

The sound of water screeching to a boil
reminds me of my grandmother's
trembling hand pouring her steam hissing

kettle over the Lipton's teabag settled
in her white porcelain cup.
Those would be the mornings I'd have slept over

on the pull-out in the living room, bundled in flannel,
watching lights from traffic below make angels on the ceiling.
My grandfather would already be out for the day,

picking up a nice brisket, a few carrots, nodding
to shopkeepers on his walk down Broadway, picking
the wrong horses at the corner OTB. He'd only bet ponies

with the same name as one of his daughters, or grandchildren,
a horse with a name that started with *K* or *J, S* or *N.*
In the evening I'd watch grownups as if studying another species:

Gretel with her bargains, *I got this sweater for ninety-nine cents!*
Catherine the milliner, hat pins sticking out of the sides of her mouth.
Why did my grandmother hide money in a drawer

under the kitchen table? How was she able
to put her red lipstick on without a mirror, never going
out of the lines? Who was Uncle Joe? Why'd she shriek

at my grandfather when he returned from the store
without the dill after dark because he'd forgotten his way home?
Why did he never say anything back, but just look at me

sitting at the fold out card table where I'd been waiting all day to watch
him rip the cellophane off a new Bicycle deck, break it open, shuffle, *let's
play, I've got a hand like a foot*, he'd always say.

THEY ONLY WANT MEATLOAF

I offered them everything:
coq au vin, skirt steak, lettuce cups
overflowing with pork and mint,

but they wanted none of it.
I offered them all of me:
dancing on a table with scarves,

spread out under a bridge,
water rising inch by inch,
but they wanted none of it.

I offered them a walk around
the ledge of a moonlit sky,
wedge darkness between their toes,

but no, no . . . I gave them one invitation
after another to discover
hidden rooms inside their dreams,

wrestle the echo of their screams
as the fire burned closer and we fell asleep,
folded into each other's arms—

but they only want meatloaf—
a meal to sustain them:
the simplest dish I could never provide.

THERE WILL BE THINGS YOU DO

you won't know why.
Maybe waiting to tie
your shoelaces

until everything else
is in place.
Could be you'll slide

your egg yolks aside
eat every bit of bacon,
toast, whites while the forsaken

yellow orbs stare at you
from the side pocket
of your empty plate.

People will ask
why do you save
your yolks for last

and you won't know—
won't recall
the cousin from the south

came to visit one summer
ate his eggs so odd
your family said

stuck with you
like the way
you love to be kissed

on the back of your neck
can vaguely recollect
your mother's kisses

after your bath
too gentle for memory.
There will be things you do

you won't know why
like the way you look
up at the sky

when anxious or blue
it's what your father
used to do

every family trip
when nothing else
was right

except those clouds
moving north by northwest
through the night

he showed you
what pilots knew:
factors for safe flying

are visibility
and how low
and mean the clouds are.

MINOR TREMORS

Family photos slanted
on the wall
must have shifted
after a small quake
I never felt
the impact of
I only remember that big one
shaking us awake at 4:00 a.m.
the two of us
trying to balance our way
along rippling floorboards
palms flat against the wall
our bodies hurled
down the long hall
struggling against the obscene
force of earth
to retrieve our son
sleeping in his crib

Can't put my finger on
the years
of minor tremors
between then and now
but I know things have changed
When did the cup on the top shelf
topple to its side
when did the hairline

fracture on the living room wall
become a crack spreading across the ceiling
When did I feel the shift
in my heart
They say the small ones
relieve the pressure
so the big one won't come
Still, every time I feel a truck
rumble through the alley
I brace myself
for the ground to finally open
I'm ready to slip away
into its burning core

SELF-PORTRAIT WITH IMAGINARY BROTHER

after de Kooning

My imaginary brother is not made of charcoal and ink,
living on paper. He is made of ashes and dust, particles of light
breathing down through the night.

Gone before he was ever born, I've only heard about him
how he would have been the first, miscarried by my mother.
He was too young to care, but I know

he exists out there in the air because sometimes I feel a kiss
but no one's there. I want to believe that if he'd been born,
he'd have pulled me in a wagon

through the park in a storm. He'd have guarded my room
wearing shields and armor, helped the rest of us learn to be calmer.
I wonder does my mother

ever think of him now—her first she never had?
And, though she has me and my other brother, would she have
loved him more, and would I

have looked more like the other, my imaginary brother,
the one who'd have taught me to swim through the ocean in a storm?
In my self-portrait with imaginary brother,

we sit in a field facing one another.
Painted in bright colors, oil and acrylic on board,
my hair is pink, my lips are black; we each hold a sword.

MOTHER'S DAY

They all climb into her bed bringing breakfast lunch and dinner.
All her children, her friends with children, their children,
her mother, her mother's mother, the daughters she never had,
the ones with long hair she never spent hours braiding.

They are all naked except for scarves which they wear on their heads
or covering their shoulders, or tied around their waists.
It's Mother's Day and they're ready to celebrate.
Who's hungry, her mother asks all the mothers and their children?

We are all hungry, they say, as they grab the hardboiled eggs
jiggling in a blue ceramic bowl in the middle of the bed. *We are all
thirsty, too*, say the little ones, holding up their sippy cups,
their scarves sliding off their heads, their mothers ferociously

tying knots that won't slip under their chins. Her mother's mother
is so old she doesn't know it's Mother's Day. She doesn't ever remember
not being a mother, has sweet butter in her veins, has made so many
beds she doesn't know why she's in this one. *Who are all these people,*

she asks one of the unknown children. *I don't know*, says the little boy.
*I don't want my scarf. I left my robot in my room and I forgot to turn him off.
He's probably left the house, on his way to the park or maybe back to Jupiter, or
getting ice cream. My mother is taking too long and I want to go home.*

she's not really dead. Pink Dot Free Delivery,
new Discover Card, The Democratic Party—
when something arrives for her in my box,
which is where her mail's been forwarded,
I open it, read it to her so she knows
people are still inquiring. Better insurance,
a chance to cast her vote, a letter from her
secret love. It's still all happening without her.
As long as my mother keeps getting mail
she is still alive! I reinstate her membership
to AARP so they will send a free insulated
tote bag, which I will keep for me. Even alive
she'd never have used it—liked to walk hands
free. She'll never know I stole it. She won't be mad
because she's dead. I've finally accepted the fact
that some things aren't meant for the recipient
but for the interceptor: the one in surgical gloves
who sees the tumor, removes, buries it, the one
who eliminates the unprotected truth.

TIME OF ARRIVAL

I called my mother last night
to tell her my plane had landed,
I'd be home for dinner, but she
wasn't there. She was there,
like on the phone, but she wasn't
there there. I kept saying, mom,
can you hear me, the plane has landed,
I'll be home for dinner, but she
said nothing. I could see her face,
could see her holding the phone,
an old fashioned one, yellow coiled cord,
her head tilted, her sunny smile, but
her voice was barely discernable. I get
that she's dead, but we had a ritual—
always reported when one another landed.
My mother and I. We had a ritual.

THIRST

My father never saw my house
though without his modest savings
we never could have bought it.

My father didn't know his grandson
past the age of ten, but today at twenty-eight
my boy has his eyes

and many of his talents. My father
died thirsty. We couldn't fill
his needs; no one could.

He had a big personality, my mother
would say, sucked the air
out of a room, needed you to pay

attention to his every word, a wall
of talk we wanted to jump over.
My father could tell a good

joke, do the accents, had the timing.
Why wasn't *that* appreciated.
He could sell anything, untangle a knot

out of the most delicate chain.
His stuff looked nice, his paintings framed.
He'd serve pats of butter on a dish

restaurant style. Our people leave us
and we let them go. They fade
into the tapestry of the dead,

an occasional memory slapping us
in the face tapping us on the shoulder
kissing the breeze by our cheek.

We wait for the wind to blow
these reminders, like it did for me today,
just now, in my garden that he never saw,

but would have loved, even though my roses
are struggling, their white petals dropping
so thirsty they are; so ready for a drink.

MY MOTHER BAKES SUGAR COOKIES

My mother bakes sugar cookies
in Heaven which is funny
because she never baked
here on earth.

They have you doing that
first thing, she told me

They have you baking
right away so you'll feel useful
we deliver the cookies
to children who've passed

The people in charge of Heaven
sound so thoughtful, I tell her.
Well, they're angels,
she says,

but not like you'd imagine.
Sure, they wear white,
have wings,
smile sweetly

but they all talk way too much,
and their asses
are huge.

WHY WE DREAM

My mother has been dead for ten months
but last night I dreamed she was alive
and we met somewhere in LA, nowhere
I'd ever been before, it was hilly more
like San Francisco, clear air everywhere,
and she had long, straight, thick red hair,
nothing like her no-hair before she died.
She was wearing my black cashmere coat,
too big for me so I gave it to my aunt
in real life, one fall trip back to New York.
When I told my mother that I gave it to my aunt
she was mad then happy because it made me
a nice person and proved she'd been a good mother.
I said in my dream, *mom, you look so young,*
so new—her evening gloves chic sliding under
the softness of the coat, her beret slanted
just so, her forties' movie star smile, lots of teeth,
dimples, lipstick and charm—*I'm not dead,*
she said, *I'm going to the Opera!* This is the kind
of dream that helps me live with the nightmares.

WE TOOK OFF IN THE SNOW

Flew up into white air everywhere
white into grey smoke through the bright
curtain of sun streaming down
through the cold meeting blue
We're safe now the snow
falls only below
Up here we no longer care
My toddler son sucks
his yellow plastic butterfly
seatbelt tight as the plane
reaches cruising I sip vodka on ice
lick salt from my fingers greasy from nuts
This is a family trip
My husband sits further back
seat 32A I turn to give him the *ok,*
we're fine up here more steady
than we are on the ground
where life changes as fast as our son's moods
where we don't believe in Heaven
not like up here where I just
saw it peek through
mountains of dunes drifting like snow
remember the snow
on the ground when we left
when you're high enough
thirty-five thousand feet new clouds will break apart
opening to a different heaven you can view

the world differently even a river
might appear as your son sleeps
your husband way in back
will close his eyes and his head will tip
touching the woman's arm next to him
she herself asleep dreaming
of the man she hasn't yet met
who'll kiss her as the clouds part
snow falling below plane cruising
my boy's lips stuck to the butterfly as I
remember long ago sitting alone in my room
listening to the traffic below waiting
to be older so I could fly away

ALTERNATIVE FLUTE

This morning she is grateful for her husband's
snoring. She wants to hear the same
sounds, things in place like always.

One more week and their only child
will leave for college. He will swap
the blue Pacific for uncertain Ohio:

she and her husband will be alone
like when they started.
She lies in bed, her mind racing

like the silver scooter
her son crisscrossed through Roxbury Park,
remembers feeding him ground turkey

and peas thawed in ice trays; dropping him off
first preschool day in a Hollywood backyard
she worried had needles in the grass.

This is a good time, some say,
the best years are to come . . .
but she thinks the best were those eighteen

that flew by in a shopping cart,
evaporated like dust in the upstairs closet
filled with his old caps and cowboy costumes.

She can still feel her breasts heavy with milk,
see his little chin lift to latch on.
Would you want him to be a baby forever?

the waxer lady asks her, ripping off stray hairs
from her bikini line, the stubborn ones
that want to hang on the way she wants

her boy to stay. *Yes*, she thinks, would give up
years of future to have one month from the past,
cuddling him during a 2:00 a.m. feeding.

College is so exciting, her friend says,
*maybe he'll take Alternative Flute, read the classics,
find himself.* In the room the women come and go . . .
trudging through the dreary snow.
Yes, he will find his *new* self, waking from a dream,
a glimmer of the ghost he was certain lived in his closet

brushing against him as he walks around the edges
of his life, tattoos on his strong arms
the only memories that can never fade.

HUGE RAT IN LAUNDRY ROOM

written on a Post-it stuck to the coffee maker
I read it first thing in the morning my son wrote it
the night he came home with his dirty clothes
dumped them in the laundry room
the rat standing in the middle of the floor next to the washer
looked up at him and when I saw the Post-it at 6:00 a.m.
I wondered why he didn't scream when he saw the rat
and how did it get in under the cabinets
you know they can shrink down to the thickness
of paper their bones collapsing like years
of memories they can slink in or out of any hole
crawl space sealed corner squeeze themselves like toothpaste
through a hair fracture in cement
I will imagine its nose bobbing around my laundry
sniffing panties in the dark
looking up at my son who came home last night
to dump his clothes have a bite to eat
sleep in the bed where he became a man

EXTRACTION

My dentist tells me it's the longest root
he's ever seen as he uses all his strength
to pull out my top back molar been hurting
since as long as I can remember feels like he's
extracting my brain forcing every thought
I ever had out of my head longest root he said
my mouth so numb I have no mouth
the tooth doesn't want to leave its warm
dysfunctional socket headquarters from where
it's been tormenting me for years lighthouse of pain
tooth that reminds me everyday that everything's
not okay let me see its calcified pulp let me roll it
in my fingers remember being a girl alone
in the dentist's waiting room reading stories
in *Newsweek* about the soldiers coming home
man on the moon get the tooth out remove
this neon time bomb red alert tooth depleting
my good will let me worship it for showing me
what hurts can be removed will end let me
wear it around my neck to prove even roots
that have fused can be ripped out

PROGRESS

Upstairs in the room
where my son used to live
I hear a stampede of animals
charging the roof, right above
where his head used to be.
I hear so many of them, God knows
what they are: squirrels, elephants, rats
for sure. He'd be scared up there,
that's what he said, and now I know why.
I worry these creatures might crawl
through the open widows, getting
louder overhead as I lay on the bed
like he did trying to fall asleep
after a long day at school, football,
the things they do we can never really
understand. I'm listening to my neighbor
talk on the phone; can hear his side
of the conversation, her side, too,
seems so intrusive but I can't stop
and probably my son listened, too, heard
the old married couple who moved away,
used to get high, sing old songs on the piano,
what did he think of them—were they a comfort
or a freak show, a window into what his parents
might become. I don't remember thinking anything
when I was fourteen except when can I
get out of here, as I studied my mother,

her friends, how they moved their mouths,
how their lips would curl down
when they spoke of their husbands.
This is what we do. This is the only way
we can understand our own species, shake
the dead off our bodies, invite ourselves
into the new world of ourselves.

We are like no one else in the world,

the killer's mother says
as she asks the victims to feel
her prayers

imagine her pain
looking at photos of the bodies
a dull knife
slicing into her belly

what song to sing
what blue sky
sweet air
can ever be hers
what's left
but to mourn
wish her son
was never born

if not for her
there'd be no baby
she held, comforted
fed with a spoon
no baby to turn

what poison
had she passed into her womb
the undecorated room

where his fingers grew long enough
to fit the trigger so well

what was she thinking
the day his brain formed
as he lay curled inside her
the time bomb gene
melting under his tongue

he could have been
my son

LATE SEPTEMBER

7:11 p.m., dark again
as daylight, reluctant felon
turns itself in

We tread water at dusk
ask the moon to forgive us

remember when
we were about to begin

and spring broke out in a sweat
all of us on the steps
late evening sunsets
now a memory
as we ease into
the starched white pillow
of winter

This hurts my back,
my father would say
late July days at the beach
when he'd reach beneath the kelp
scoop us kids out of the ocean

We didn't care
about our father's pain
our mother's boredom

just wanted more
of the same—staying up late

party cake, loving the sun
for telling the moon to get lost
as we'd be tossed

by the waves
runaways, ice cream and sand
crusted between our hungry fingers

DAUGHTER SUSPECTS DEAD MOTHER
OF STEALING HER SHOES

My shoes are missing.
I looked on the bottom of my closet
and none are there. Not the boots
you loved me to wear, the ones that tied up
crisscross always came undone,
not the simple black pumps I saved for work.
Did you take them? We can share, you know,
I'm fine with that, I loved the ones you wore
to the wedding, remember, black patent
leather, simple bow. The red ones I never
liked. *Ostentatious*, Nana said.
People will see your shoes before they see
you, and what good is that?
I will leave the house now, my bare feet
poised for the cold or heat, my toes
digging into the moist soil where I once
planted the pit from an avocado we had for lunch.
There was plenty of sun back there.
Something should have grown.

Would you donate your brain to science,

the stranger in the linen department of Macy's
asks me? I look around to be sure she's talking
to me. *I don't know, would you?* I reply,
not knowing what else to say, what really can
one say? Maybe this person has already
donated her brain to science and that's why
she's asking me this question. *I'm thinking
about it,* she says. *I wish I could donate it
while I'm still alive so they could tell me why
I need to move objects around on my desk,
why I can never settle on the perfect shade of red,
why I can't accept love. I have a brain,"* I tell her,
"*and I'm holding onto it.* I want to see if it will
deteriorate on its own, organically like my mother's,
leaving me unabashedly knowing what I want:
no excuses, denial, shame, debate, just silence,
shh, a moment to feel the thrill of only what I need:
tissues, a breeze, macaroni and cheese.
At last I will be the perfect gift to myself.

CRANKY IN PARADISE

she's at their beach house
aqua and peach on all sides
air sweet enough to pour over pancakes

wet life crawling under her
breaking through the mound of hard
sand she built to rest her head

waves striking every few minutes like
contractions before birth
she rubs her belly hands cold

the deck above shaking with fun-lovers
reminds herself this day will end
but she won't know why

it hurt so much why she was lost
as the milky foam
chasing her away from the shore

she feels the beat of conversation
mixed with the rhythm of the sea
what are they saying up there?

closes her eyes deep breath scent of seaweed
she's fading now counts backwards like when
they took her tonsils out or when they took her

baby out when nothing else mattered
but the sound of their own hearts
and paradise was nothing more than being alive

WHILE WASHING THE DINNER DISHES

Tonight as I washed the knife
I wondered what it'd be like
to cut my arm off

right below the shoulder, saw back
and forth through tendon,
fibrous tissue, deep

into muscle, red spurting down
onto the hardwood floor,
my dog licking it up,

wondered how that much blood
would smell, how otherworldly
the pain would be,

white screeches inside bone.
I imagined what fine dinner
party conversation it would make,

me with only one arm, *no I can't help
clear the table, I only have one arm,
I cut the other off after I washed the knife,*

and people would be shocked,
demand to know why I did it, what was I
thinking, what happened to the arm

when it hit the ground, and I'd tell them
my dog carried it off in his teeth,
tried to bury it under the tomato plants,

dug for hours, but the soil wouldn't give,
so he flung it over the fence into the crazy
people's yard.

This is what I imagined while washing the knife
at sunset, looking out the window,
watching the summer sky turn

the color of dried blood, color of secrets
my mother once shared years before
I could hear them.

SCRAMBLING EGGS

When you scramble eggs,
I show my daughter as I pour
the raw liquid onto the readied pan,
it doesn't matter whether you go slow
gently fold them into the heat
or snap your wrist—flip them over
faster than the flame
the taste of the eggs,
the memory of having eaten them,
will be the same. I don't have
a daughter, but this morning
when scrambling my eggs
deliberately, not hurriedly
as I usually do, I thought
if I had a daughter
this is what I'd tell her.
I'd wait until she was seven
and remind her again at twenty-one.
This is one of the things
I'd want her to know.

FONTANELLE

He's so lucky
the brain doctors
tell me, huddled in white
their names embroidered

in blue script across
their chests, my grown son
sprawled across the hospital bed
tubes, needles sticking

into his body, twined
around him like veins
through a parched leaf.
I can't look at him

his mouth crusted
unfocused eyes
that yesterday lit up
the room, now his skull

fractured, same head
I used to hold in one hand
his legs rocking my arm
to sleep. Infants' heads

are so soft, easy
to rupture, brains still

forming. I can't look at him now
his giant hands, filth baked

under his nails
from scratching the gutter
where he fell off
the back of a car—

of course he shouldn't have
been sitting on the trunk
of a car—but you see
they will do things

they will do things
that can hurt and we have to watch
and when I see him in that bed
hooked up to machines beeping

instructions to the nurse
making noise like garbage trucks
on collection day
I have to look away

cover my eyes like he did
when he was three
afraid to see
the flying monkeys

in *The Wizard of Oz,*
he'd run screaming
into my lap. Where is it now
The Emerald City?

Where can I get the courage
to uncover my eyes
see the blood
ooze from his ear

walk over to the bed
whisper, *I'm here, it'll be ok*
you're lucky, the doctors say
but all I can think

is what if it hadn't
gone this way—
luck, the slippery slope
of miracles, unpredictable

fragile as a fontanelle
soft luck running out
from the moment
we're born.

BOOB JOB

for my mother

Trying on clothes in the backroom
of Loehmann's, a stranger invites me
to feel her breasts, a stranger trying on
dresses that don't fit and I can see
her breasts are larger than they want
to be, and she can see I'm watching,
asks me to help zip her up and I struggle
to pull her in, smooth out her sunburned skin,
tug, ask her to shake herself in, she tells me
she just got them, didn't know they'd come out
so big isn't sure she likes them, not even her
husband cares, *he's not a breast man*, she says,
he's an ass man but I'm not getting an ass job,
good, I say, because how do you even *get* an ass job,
do you want to feel them, she asks, and I do, so I do
and they feel like bean bags you'd toss at a clown's face
at a kid's party, I squeeze them both at the same time,
cup my hands underneath them, she says, *go ahead*,
squeeze some more, it's not sexual, aren't they heavy,
I don't want to have them around every day, her nipples
headlights staring into the dressing room mirror, red scars
around their circumferences, angry circles I want to run
my finger around, *you should have seen them before*
I had them lifted, they were long drooping points,
couldn't stand looking at them anymore, can I see yours,
so I show her, so small hers could eat mine alive,
nipples like walnuts, do you think I should make mine

bigger, and there we are examining one another's boobs,
touching, talking about them like they aren't there,
don't matter, forgetting how it felt when we were twelve
or thirteen, one morning when they first appeared
sore, swollen, exciting, new, when they had the power
to turn us into women we no longer knew.

THANKING MY BREASTS

I want to take this opportunity
to thank my breasts for being
such good sports, still perky
after so many let downs, still
happy to meet new people,
willing to try new things.
When they first arrived, way before
my friends had theirs, we had some fun
jumping up and down on my bed, lying
on my side to feel them squish together,
the miracle of cleavage. I'd imagine
I was Ann-Margret in *Bye Bye Birdie*,
hold my pink princess phone,
watch them in the mirror watch me
as I flirted with a pretend boyfriend.
They tormented Mr. Johnson, my pervy
flute teacher, were felt up by Angel
at Phil's Pizza on Broadway, took me
to bed at night crying to be touched.
They hadn't a clue how far we'd go together—
how many padded bras I'd shake them into,
release them from. There was that scare
when I was twenty—an overnight at Doctor's
Hospital, anesthesia, biopsy, stitches, pressure
bandage covering my left nipple like an eye patch,
damp with sweat that long, humid summer.
But that was that; only a wisp of a scar remains,

pale as a thinning hair, undecipherable
to even the smoothest lips. They got smaller as I
got older, but a man I love tells me they're pretty.
They fed my son those glorious first eighteen months,
and when the milk was gone, their new life began.
They had no friends, no other breasts to talk to,
but they always had me, still do, and right now
we're going to take a walk in the park.

DAMAGE

My mother was careful not to fall,
chose each step as deliberately
as she chose her words, each one
straightened in place like her half slip.

I thought of her before dawn
when I walked up my narrow stairs
in the dark holding my coffee and a stack
of books. I almost tripped, remembered

how careful she was, would never put
herself in jeopardy, didn't want an injury,
would never carry a high stack of books
and coffee filled to the brim

up a narrow staircase in the dark, but this
is how we're different, I can be reckless,
impulsive, spurt out, fall in love, ruin a day
with one wrong step, drop a platter of cold cuts

onto the wet grass seconds before presenting
to my guests, can fall off the roof of a sidewalk,
back up into the side of a truck, let a word slide
out of my mouth like a rusty razor blade,

let myself fall for the impossible. Oh the puddles
I've stepped in, the hairs I've allowed to go
down the drain, the parts of myself I've swept
to the curb, some still moving.

GIFT CABINET

Hot and muggy this August morning in LA
and I wake with my hair damp, matted
on the back of my neck, falls uninspired
onto my shoulders. I recall how my mother
would lift my hair up, *darling, get your hair
off your neck*, she'd brush and pull it so tight
into a ponytail my temples would crack.
The rubber band she used was red, the one
that had wrapped the celery, no scrunchies
back then. I never liked her to touch my hair,
unlike other daughters who may have craved
that sort of attention, hair so thick and long
it felt intimate, mine alone, keep your hands off.
As I sit at my table this airless Saturday,
a small package is tossed into the front yard.
It's from Nancy, an old friend in the Bay,
hair heavier, more complicated than mine.
I wonder if she's feeling hot, too, those fires
raging not far from where she lives, if she's pulled
her hair away from her face, if her mother
got too involved like mine did. Not much, I think,
can change the direction of this day, but inside the box
is a Rainbow Maker, a colorful little machine
with a crystal that promises to create
beautiful rainbows that move around the room.
She found it in her gift cabinet, thought of me.
Once in a great while, something like this

might happen. It's all it takes to bring back breathable air.

HANDS

I look down at my hands
as I scrub for the necessary twenty
seconds, twenty becoming thirty, thirty
becoming longer as I'm lulled
by watching my fingers, thinking
how much my hands now look
like my mother's—capable, strong,
nails cut down, unpolished.
What would she think about COVID-19?
Would she wash as diligently, wear
a mask to the grocery, and what
would I do if my mother were still alive,
living alone? We'd talk on the phone,
she'd retell the story of the Great
Depression, how she'd hold her little
sister's hand on the subway, how
they didn't have any spending money,
just two apples in a bag. She'd tell me
about her ration books filled with stamps.
It was the norm back then, she'd say,
not knowing what food would be found.
Where can we go to escape our hands
and the thoughts that possess us
as we scrub between our fingers?
I think of my mother's hands.
I think of the time she visited me
at my first apartment, how we slept

in the same bed and I woke up to feel
her hand on my arm, how I shook it off
and rolled over. I think about her hands
at the end, in the home, how she would
put them over mine and squeeze.
How I let her keep them there.

TELL ME

for Baudelaire

Tell me, mysterious stranger,
whom do you love the best:
your mother, your wife
your daughter, or your lover?

I have neither wife nor daughter
my mother has passed,
my lover has vanished. I have only
the vague scent of her perfume
infused in my skin.

Your country?
I cannot love what I do not trust.

Your friends?
Friends are for the young.

Then tell me, whom do you love?

I love the moon,
the moon that changes
with the whims
of the earth. I love
how it pulls me
to where I will never reach,
how the stars

cry out for its attention,
protect its glaring pain.

I love the moon
how it empties its shine
into morning.

AFTER THE RAIN

After the rain relents,
this sun feels nice on my back,
reminds me that although the dead
are gone, the way we think of them
can change. *It's always pouring in heaven,*
my mother tells me.
She comes to me in the middle
of the night, tells me
there's a cloud burst every day,
takes us by surprise, she says, *so many of us outside*
playing golf, backgammon, floating in the infinity pool.
She's lying.
Making all this Heaven shit up.
I'm not even sure she's *in* Heaven.
Here on earth my mother would embellish her stories:
add a robbery, lover, trip to Africa.
She never went to Africa, though she had many lovers,
and was robbed
a couple of times. Listen,
the sun on my back feels nice.
Why can't I just leave it that way?

WHAT WE LEAVE BEHIND

When he turned sixty-five, my father
gave me a key to his safe deposit.
Go there after I die, he said, you
and your brother, and you'll see
what I've left you. Ten years later
I found the key in a velvet pouch
where I kept my grandmother's
thin white gold wedding band.
He'd left us a little bit of money
and I cried knowing how hard
he must have worked to save it.
My mother handwrote her will
on a yellow lined pad in her fine
cursive: *Whatever I have, darling,
is yours and your brother's—*
the painting of chrysanthemums
my father did before they divorced,
a photo album filled with people
I didn't know, a serving platter
that slid from my hands,
shattered on the floor. Yesterday
I took my son up a mountain
and showed him the land below.
When I go, I told him, *this will all
be yours! The wildflowers, trees,
brown earth, yours! Look up*, I said.
The sky and clouds, above—yours!

The stars—I'm leaving those for you, too.
And, sweetheart, my biggest surprise—
the moon. The moon will always
light you in darkness, take you home.
Nothing like surprising your children
with things they never knew
would one day be theirs.

ACKNOWLEDGMENTS

Heartfelt thanks and endless gratitude to Kate Gale, Mark E. Cull, and the dedicated team of Red Hen Press, and to the editors of the following journals and publications in which these poems first appeared:

2011 Poem of the Month Calendar (Silverton Books): "Game Over"; *Air Kissing on Mars* (Red Hen Press 2010): "Alternative Flute," "Birth," "Different Mothers," "Huge Rat in Laundry Room," "The Gene," "The Couple Next Door," "The Things I Do in My Car"; *Arroyo Monthly*: "My Mother Bakes Sugar Cookies," "Scrambling Eggs"; *Barrow Street*: "Bottled Water"; *Coiled Serpent: Poets Arising from the Cultural Quakes & Shifts in Los Angeles* (Tia Chucha Press 2016): "Fontanelle" (as "Fontanel"); *Eclipse*: "Board and Care Clock"; *Glimpse Poetry Magazine*: "Hands," "What We Leave Behind"; *Interlitq*: "After the Rain," "Gift Cabinet"; *James Dickey Review*: "Damage"; *Last Train to the Missing Planet* (Red Hen Press 2016): "As long as my mother keeps getting mail," "Dying is Not Black," "Easter Sunday," "Goodbye to James Garner," "Lunch with Gloria," "Minor Tremors," "Mother's Day," "Pregnant," "Self-Portrait with Imaginary Brother," "Sleep Over," "Tell Me," "There will be things you do," "Time of Arrival," "Visiting Eleanor," "We Took Off in the Snow," "Why We Dream," "Would you donate your brain to science,"; *Los Angeles Review*: "Fontanelle" (as "Fontanel"); *Plume*: "Thanking My Breasts"; *Rattle*: "Boob Job," "The Delivery Man," "How was your weekend," "I wore this dress today for you, mom," "Letter to My Son"; *Santa Barbara Literary Journal*: "Late September"; *Slice of Moon* (Red Hen Press 2013): "Clive Christian No. 1," "Gail Explains about My Mother's Glasses," "I Lost My Mother at Bloomingdales," "Little Glass Dishes," "My Mother Has a Fitful Sleep," "My Mother Wants Extra Crisp Bacon," "No One Bleeds Forever," "Sardines," "Slice of Moon," "Solace," "The Salvation Army Won't Take the Futon," "They Only Want Meatloaf," "While Washing the Dinner Dishes"; *Solstice Magazine*: "Thirst"; *Sunbathing on Tyrone Power's Grave* (Red Hen Press 2019): "Daughter Suspects Dead Mother of Stealing Her Shoes," "Dubonnet," "Everybody Loves Dinner," "Progress," "She's never trusted happiness," "We are like no one else in the world"; *Two Hawks Quarterly*: "The People in the Health Food Store"; and *Wide Awake: Poets of Los Angeles and Beyond* (Pacific Coast Poetry Series): "Boob Job," "Extraction."

ABOUT THE AUTHOR

Kim Dower, City Poet Laureate of West Hollywood from October 2016–October 2018, and originally from New York City, has published four collections of poetry: *Air Kissing on Mars*, her first—"sensual and evocative . . . seamlessly combining humor and heartache," (*Los Angeles Times*)—was chosen as one of the few poetry books to be honored by the state of California and is on display at the Governor's Mansion; *Slice of Moon*, "unexpected and sublime," (*O Magazine*); *Last Train to the Missing Planet*, "poems that speak about the gray space between tragedy and tenderness, memory and loss, fragility and perseverance," (Richard Blanco); and *Sunbathing on Tyrone Power's Grave*, which won the Gold Ippy Award for best poetry book from an indie press in 2019. Her poems are included in several anthologies, notably, *Wide Awake: Poets of Los Angeles and Beyond*, (Beyond Baroque Books/Pacific Coast Poetry Series). She teaches workshops for Antioch University, UCLA Writer's Extension, and the West Hollywood Library. Additionally, Kim's literary publicity company, Kim-from-L.A., helps authors around the country get the word out about their wonderful books.

CPSIA information can be obtained
at www.ICGtesting.com
Printed in the USA
LVHW111944240722
723903LV00001B/1